BLAZERS

The Best of the Best

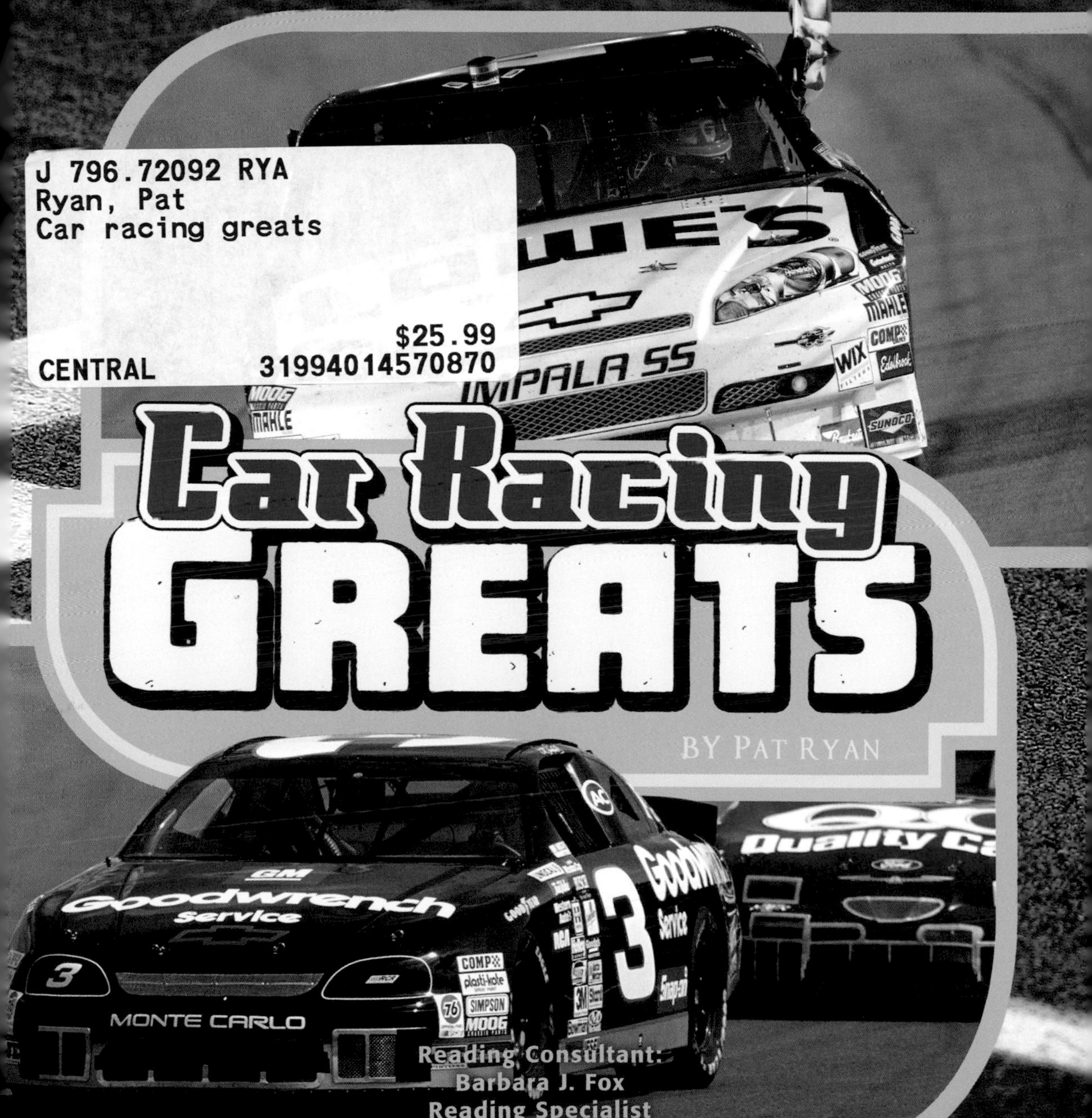

Car Racing GREATS

BY PAT RYAN

Reading Consultant:
Barbara J. Fox
Reading Specialist
North Carolina State University

CAPSTONE PRESS
a capstone imprint

Blazers is published by Capstone Press,
151 Good Counsel Drive, P.O. Box 669, Mankato, Minnesota 56002.
www.capstonepub.com

 Books published by Capstone Press are manufactured with paper
containing at least 10 percent post-consumer waste.

Library of Congress Cataloging-in-Publication Data
Ryan, Pat.
    Car racing greats / by Pat Ryan.
    p. cm. — (Blazers. best of the best)
    Includes bibliographical references and index.
    Summary: "Lists and describes top race car drivers from both the past and today"—Provided
by publisher.
    ISBN 978-1-4296-6500-1 (library binding)
    ISBN 978-1-4296-7245-0 (paperback)
    1. Automobile racing—History—Juvenile literature. I. Title. II. Series.
GV1029.R97 2012
796.72092'2—dc22
[B]   2011002462

Editorial Credits
Mandy Robbins, editor; Kyle Grenz, designer; Eric Manske, production specialist

Photo Credits
AP Images, cover (bottom); Dreamstime: Actionsports, 14-15; Getty Images for NASCAR: Rusty Jarrett, 4-5,
Tom Whitmore, cover (top); Getty Images Inc.: Clive Mason, 22-23, Dozier Mobley, 6-7, Focus on Sport,
8-9, Jeff Gross, 18-19, John Harrelson, 20-21, Jonathan Ferrey, 16-17, 24-25, Massimo Bettiol, 26-27, Racing
Photo Archives, 12-13, Stephen Dunn, 1 (top), WireImage/Allen Kee, 1 (bottom); ISC Archives via Getty
Images: RacingOne, 10-11; Landov: CSM/Scott Sewell, 29

Artistic Effects
Shutterstock: Factor41

The publisher does not endorse products whose logos may appear on objects in images in this book.

Printed in the United States of America in Stevens Point, Wisconsin.
032011   006111WZF11

TABLE OF CONTENTS

Start YOUR Engines!

Race car drivers push cars to their limits. Great racers combine speed and skill as they chase the checkered flag.

FACT The first car race was held in France in 1895.

Richard Petty
(1937-)

Richard Petty's amazing **NASCAR** career earned him the nickname "The King." He won a **record** 200 NASCAR races and seven points championships.

CLASS ACT!

NASCAR
the National Association for Stock Car Auto Racing; it is the top class of stock car racing

record—when something is done better than anyone has ever done it before

FACT Today the NASCAR points championship is called the Sprint Cup. In the past it has been called the Winston Cup (1971–2003) and the Nextel Cup (2004–2007).

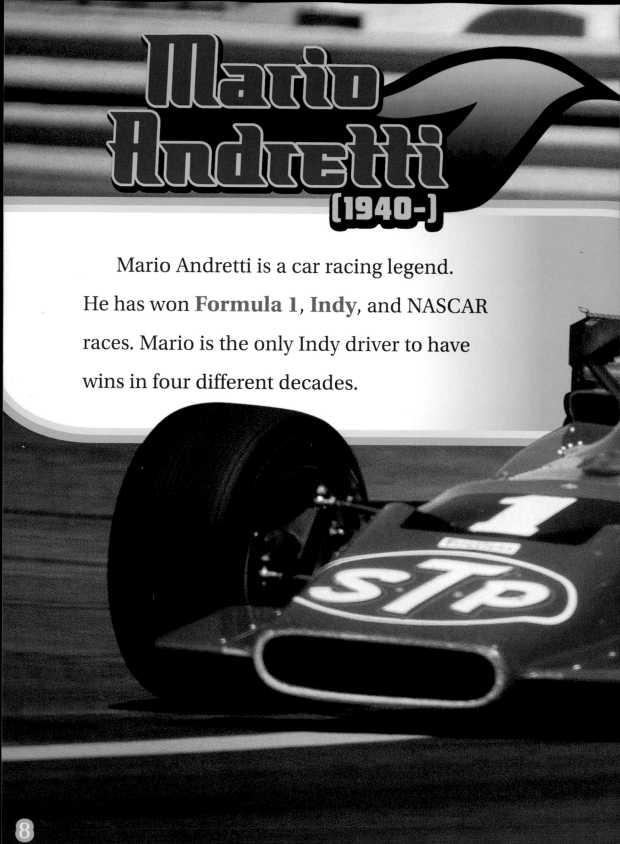

Mario Andretti (1940-)

Mario Andretti is a car racing legend. He has won **Formula 1**, **Indy**, and NASCAR races. Mario is the only Indy driver to have wins in four different decades.

CLASS ACT!

FORMULA 1
the top class of racing for Formula I race cars, a light, quick type of open-wheeled car

INDY
the top class of racing for Indy cars, a powerful type of open-wheeled car

9

A.J. Foyt

(1935-)

FACT A.J. won the 24 Hours of Le Mans and the Indianapolis 500 in 1967. He is the only driver to have won both races in the same year.

A.J. Foyt is one of Indy racing's top drivers of all time. His rough style also drew fans to stock car racing in the 1960s. A.J. has won 12 championships in different **classes** of racing.

class—a level of racing involving specific types of vehicles and racing rules

Dale Earnhardt Sr.

(1951-2001)

Dale Earnhardt Sr. drove his black #3 Monte Carlo to seven NASCAR points championships. He tied Richard Petty's record. Dale's death during the 2001 Daytona 500 shocked the racing world.

FACT Dale started racing in 1970. His first race car was a pink 1956 Ford.

Dale Earnhardt Jr.

(1974-)

Dale Earnhardt Jr., or "Junior," was born to race. He was voted Most Popular Driver seven times. Junior has won more than 15 NASCAR races, including the 2004 Daytona 500.

FACT Junior has appeared in music videos for musicians such as Sheryl Crow, Jay-Z, and Kid Rock.

Jeff Gordon
(1971-)

Jeff Gordon is a four-time NASCAR points champion. He was the first driver to reach $100 million in career winnings. Jeff has won more than 80 races, and he's not finished yet.

FACT Jeff won a national go-kart championship at age 8.

FACT In 2010 Jimmie was voted NASCAR's Driver of the Year for the third time.

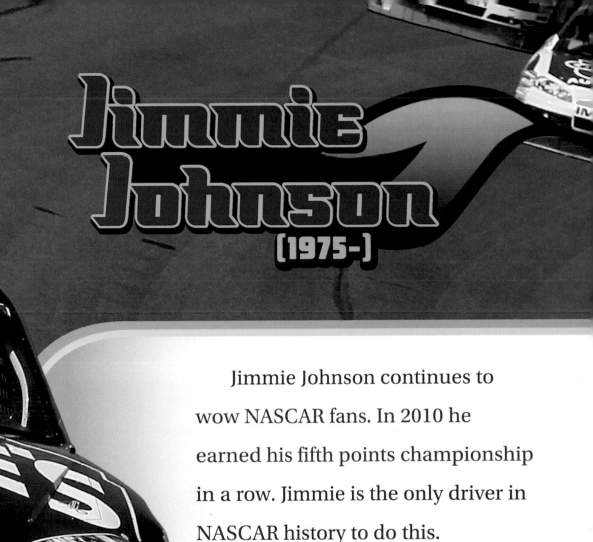

Jimmie Johnson
(1975-)

Jimmie Johnson continues to wow NASCAR fans. In 2010 he earned his fifth points championship in a row. Jimmie is the only driver in NASCAR history to do this.

Kurt Busch
(1978-)

FACT Kurt began racing dwarf cars when he was 15.

Kurt Busch has raced almost every kind of vehicle. In 2004 he won the NASCAR points championship. Kurt continues to be a threat on the track.

Michael Schumacher

(1969-)

Michael Schumacher may be the greatest Formula 1 driver ever. Schumacher has won the most **pole positions** and the most races. No one has beaten his record of seven World Championship wins.

pole position–the inside spot in the front row of cars at the beginning of a race

Danica Patrick

(1982-)

Danica Patrick leads the way for female racers. In 2008 she won the Indy Japan 300. She became the first woman to win an Indy car race. Danica started racing in NASCAR races in 2010.

FACT Danica won the 2008 Kids' Choice Award for favorite female athlete.

Sebastien Loeb

(1974-)

Sebastien Loeb won seven **World Rally Car** championship titles in a row. Sebastien's control on snow and dirt has brought him a record 61 wins.

FACT Rally car racing is an event in the X Games. This action sports competition is held every year.

CLASS ACT!

WORLD RALLY CAR
the top class of rally car racing, a type of long-distance racing covering many types of terrain

John Force
(1949-)

John Force is a drag racing legend. He has won 15 **Funny Car** Championships. John also has 129 career wins.

CLASS ACT!

FUNNY CAR
a class of racing for a specific type of drag racing car that slows down with the help of a parachute

FACT John's three daughters, Ashley, Brittany, and Courtney, also drag race.

Glossary

career (kuh-REER)—the type of work a person does over a long period of time

class (KLASS)—a level of racing involving specific types of vehicles and racing rules

funny car (FUH-nee CAR)—a specific type of drag racer that slows down with the help of a parachute

legend (LEJ-uhnd)—someone who is among the best in what they do

pole position (POHL puh-ZISH-uhn)—the inside spot in the front row at the beginning of a race

record (REK-urd)—when something is done better than anyone has ever done it before

Read More

David, Jack. *Stock Cars.* Cool Rides. Minneapolis, Minn.: Bellwether Media, 2008.

Francis, Jim. *Great NASCAR Champions.* NASCAR New York: Crabtree Pub. Co., 2008.

Parker, Steve. *On The Race Track.* Machines Rule! Mankato, Minn.: Smart Apple Media, 2010.

Internet Sites

FactHound offers a safe, fun way to find Internet sites related to this book. All of the sites on FactHound have been researched by our staff.

Here's all you do:

Visit *www.facthound.com*

Type in this code: 9781429665001

Index